WHAT
I WANT
YOU TO
KNOW

(Or, advice you never asked for.)

GLORY BOX PRESS

TO:

FROM:

WHAT I WANT YOU TO KNOW

CHAPTER 1: LIFE SKILLS

CHAPTER 2 : ADULTING

CHAPTER 3 : ABOUT ME

CHAPTER 4 : ABOUT YOU

CHAPTER 5 : BIG EMOTIONS

CHAPTER 6 : RELATIONSHIPS

CHAPTER 7 : BEING A WHOLE PERSON

LIFE SKILLS

Top COOKING Tips

Although the secret ingredient is always love (or cheese), remember: no whisk — no reward!

Top COOKING SAFETY Tips

Cuts, burns, exploding dishes...the kitchen is a dangerous place. Stay safe with these tips!

Our SECRET FAMILY Recipe

Every family has one – that favorite dish that comes out at every family gathering. Here's ours!

The story:

Ingredients:

_____
_____
_____
_____
_____
_____
_____
_____
_____
_____
_____
_____
_____
_____
_____
_____
_____
_____

Instructions:

_____
_____
_____
_____
_____
_____
_____
_____
_____

Tips:

Your FAVORITE FOOD I make

_____

I always make this for you when:

_____
_____
_____
_____
_____
_____
_____
_____

Ingredients:

_____
_____
_____
_____
_____
_____
_____
_____
_____

Instructions:

_____

_____

_____

_____

_____

_____

_____

_____

_____

_____

_____

_____

_____

_____

_____

_____

_____

_____

_____

_____

_____

Tips:

_____

_____

_____

_____

_____

TOP KITCHEN HACKS

Graters gonna grate, but there's a lot of ways to make your kitchen life easier!

What TO CLEAN AND HOW Often

Did you know you should wash your washing machine once a month? Us neither!

Non-obvious Things
YOU NEED TO CLEAN

Ceiling fans, toilet bowl bases, game controllers ... what else are you forgetting?

Best CLEANING Hacks

While your house should be dirty enough to be happy, it should also be clean enough to be healthy!

Top HOMECARE Tips

New home, who dis? Owning or renting a home comes with a whole bunch of responsibilities you never knew existed. Fun!

| |
| |
| |
| |
| |
| |

Top HOME MAINTENANCE Hacks

Your home is your castle ... so don't let it become a ruin!

Things you should KNOW HOW TO FIX

If it ain't broke, don't fix it. But if it is....

Dealing with EMERGENCIES

What qualifies as an emergency,
and who to contact.

General HYGIENE Advice

You won't get dirty unless you're clean first!

How-to DRESS YOURSELF

Always dress to impress ... yourself!
But also:

Top BEAUTY Hacks

Kool-Aid, diaper rash cream, and paper toilet seat covers – how I get so gorgeous!

MANAGING your MONEY

Money can't buy you happiness, but no money can't buy you anything!

| |
| |
| |
| |
| |
| |

SETTING GOALS

And how to accomplish them ...

| |
| |
| |
| |
| |
| |

Tips for SURVIVING the ZOMBIE APOCALYPSE

Hey, it **could** happen.

ADULTING

ADULTING

Top HOSTING Tips

Are you going to serve food? Drinks?
Or is it just an excuse to clean the house?

| |
| |
| |
| |
| |
| |

3-Course FOOLPROOF Menu

It doesn't have to be fancy, just edible!

Theme/Occasion:

MENU

Starter:

Main:

Dessert:

STARTER

Ingredients:

_____
_____
_____
_____
_____
_____
_____
_____
_____
_____
_____
_____
_____
_____
_____
_____
_____
_____
_____

Instructions:

_____
_____
_____
_____
_____
_____
_____
_____
_____
_____
_____

Tips:

MAIN

Ingredients:

_____
_____
_____
_____
_____
_____
_____
_____
_____
_____
_____
_____
_____
_____
_____
_____
_____
_____
_____

Instructions:

_____
_____
_____
_____
_____
_____
_____
_____
_____
_____

Tips:

DESSERT

Ingredients:

_____
_____
_____
_____
_____
_____
_____
_____
_____
_____
_____
_____
_____
_____
_____
_____
_____
_____
_____
_____

Instructions:

_____
_____
_____
_____
_____
_____
_____
_____
_____
_____

Tips:

Tips for approaching YOUR CRUSH

Without looking like an unhinged stalker.

DRESSING for a DATE

The art of peacocking/henning .... or not!

DRESSING for a NIGHT OUT

For goodness sake, wear a jacket!

How to STAY SAFE on a NIGHT OUT

As much as I would prefer you to never leave the house after dark, or before dark, or, well, ... ever, we both know you will. Pay attention.

Using ALCOHOL and DRUGS

I mean, it's not like you ever would, right?
But just in case ...

How to deal with STRANGERS

For both your safety and theirs!

How to BUY GIFTS for other people

The gifts you give say a lot about you
– and who your're buying them for.

Giving and Receiving:
GIFT ETIQUETTE

Because there is an art to both!

Tips for SURVIVING SCHOOL

Because even though it's not forever,
it can certainly feel like it!

Tips for CHOOSING A CAREER

Just because it's work doesn't mean you have to hate it.

Tips for JOB INTERVIEWS

Stand out for all the right reasons!

Tips for WORKING YOUR FIRST JOB

Striking the balance between self-respect and staying employed.

WORK ETIQUETTE Advice

Spoiler alert: it's kinda like the playground.

How to NOT BE A D*CK

It's not that hard ...

Dealing with BIGOTRY

When people think ignorance is easier than understanding

Advice on BULLYING

Unhappy people want you to be miserable too.

Tips for DEALING with A**HOLES

Cuz the world is full of them.

How to treat SERVICE WORKERS

Cuz they don't need you to make their jobs any harder!

COMPETITION

It doesn't have to be a fight to the death!

Talking about POLITICS

Or, how to ruin any social gathering!

RELIGION

Religion can be as divisive as pineapple on pizza. So here is my advice:

How to have a CONVERSATION

No one will expect you to be the world's greatest conversationalist, but you should be able to hold your own!

How to ARGUE YOUR POINT

(So that people will actually listen to you)

MAKING MISTAKES

You're gonna make mistakes.
It's how you deal with them that matters.

How to APOLOGIZE

(and mean it)

INTERNET ETIQUETTE
Tips

A keyboard isn't a license to be a terrible human being.

Tips for INTERNET SAFETY

Grooming, hacking, doxxing, bullying...
Stay safe on the digital mean streets!

How to cope WHEN YOU'RE SICK

Being sick is all fun and games until you live on your own!

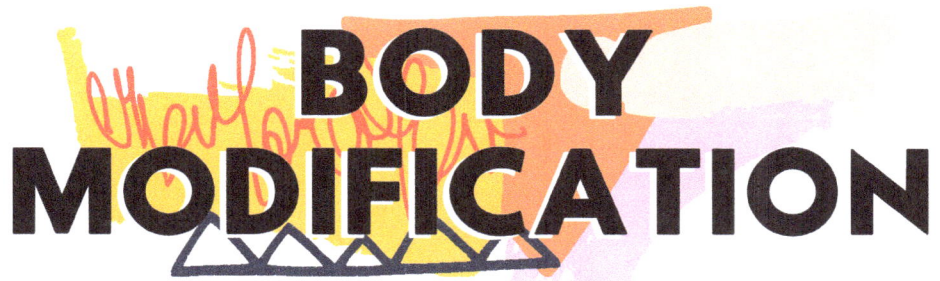

BODY MODIFICATION

and how to minimize regret.

Traveling in a FOREIGN COUNTRY

Check your privilege at the door.

<table>
<tr><td></td></tr>
<tr><td></td></tr>
<tr><td></td></tr>
<tr><td></td></tr>
<tr><td></td></tr>
<tr><td></td></tr>
</table>

My PET CARE Advice

You promised to feed it, clean up after it, and walk it four times a day? Well, now you can!

ABOUT ME

ABOUT ME

Things you might not KNOW ABOUT ME

_____
_____
_____
_____
_____
_____
_____
_____
_____
_____
_____
_____
_____
_____
_____
_____
_____
_____
_____
_____
_____
_____
_____
_____
_____
_____
_____
_____
_____
_____
_____
_____

My MISTAKES and REGRETS

Things I WANT TO APOLOGIZE for

_____
_____
_____
_____
_____
_____
_____
_____
_____
_____
_____
_____
_____
_____
_____
_____
_____
_____
_____
_____
_____
_____
_____
_____
_____
_____
_____
_____
_____
_____
_____
_____
_____

What I AM AFRAID of

Things that
SCARE ME

_____
_____
_____
_____
_____
_____
_____
_____
_____
_____
_____
_____
_____
_____
_____
_____
_____
_____
_____
_____
_____
_____
_____
_____
_____
_____
_____

What
I HOPE
FOR YOU

_____
_____
_____
_____
_____
_____
_____
_____
_____
_____
_____
_____
_____
_____
_____
_____
_____
_____
_____
_____
_____
_____
_____
_____
_____
_____
_____
_____
_____

ABOUT YOU

ABOUT YOU

things that REMIND ME OF YOU

Times YOU MADE ME PROUD

Things YOU TAUGHT ME

_____
_____
_____
_____
_____
_____
_____
_____
_____
_____
_____
_____
_____
_____
_____
_____
_____
_____
_____
_____
_____
_____
_____
_____
_____
_____
_____
_____
_____
_____

Your GREATEST STRENGTHS

_____
_____
_____
_____
_____
_____
_____
_____
_____
_____
_____
_____
_____
_____
_____
_____
_____
_____
_____
_____
_____
_____
_____
_____
_____
_____
_____
_____
_____
_____
_____
_____
_____

BIG EMOTIONS

BIG EMOTIONS

Coping with ANGER

When red is the only color you can see...

Coping with
DISAPPOINTMENT

Sometimes life will kick you in the teeth.

Coping with ANXIETY

It may be a part of you,
but it's not who you are.

Coping with STRESS

Take a deep breath....

Dealing with DEPRESSION

When you need everything to stop, just for a moment.

Surviving EMBARRASSMENT

So you can laugh about it later!

Giving and Receiving FORGIVENESS

It's a privilege, not a right.

Coping with FRUSTRATION

Fetch the screaming pillow!

Coping with GRIEF

It does get better.

Be the hero of your own story.

Dealing with JEALOUSY

Sometimes you're the prince(ss),
sometimes you're the frog.

Dealing with REGRETS

You'll have a few.

Coping with SUCCESS & FAILURE

You can learn a lot from both.

RELATIONSHIPS

RELATIONSHIPS

Showing KINDNESS

A small act for you, a huge impact for others.

How to TREAT OTHERS

Be the world you want to live in.

What to look for in a FRIEND

Surround yourself with people who will lift you up!

How to be a GOOD FRIEND

Make friendships that last a lifetime.

DATING ETIQUETTE

So much more than just chewing with your mouth closed!

What to look for in a PARTNER

Find a soulmate ... not a cellmate.

How to be a GOOD PARTNER

Hint: it's not all about you...

| |
| |
| |
| |
| |
| |

BOUNDARIES
You should set

And absolutely, 100% stick to.

| |
| |
| |
| |
| |
| |

Then run!!

My RELATIONSHIP Advice

Romeo and Juliet was **not** a romance.

My BREAKUP Advice

If they break up with you...

My BREAKUP Advice

If you break up with them ...

How to be a GOOD FAMILY Member

(Without compromising your own dreams)

<table>
<tr><td></td></tr>
<tr><td></td></tr>
<tr><td></td></tr>
<tr><td></td></tr>
<tr><td></td></tr>
<tr><td></td></tr>
</table>

Tips for LIVING with ROOMMATES

Cleaning up after yourself is just the beginning!

Tips for LIVING with your PARTNER

They're your lover ... **not** your mother!

How to be a GOOD GUEST

Don't outstay your welcome!

BEING A

WHOLE PERSON

How to FACE THE WORLD
With your mental health intact

Not impossible, but not easy either!

Tips for MENTAL Self-care

Because your most important relationship is with yourself.

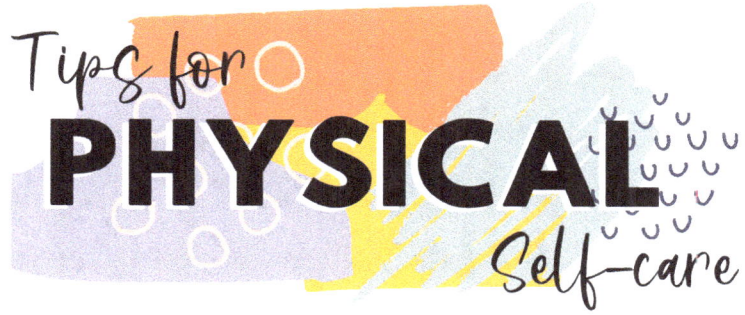

Tips for PHYSICAL Self-care

Self-care isn't selfish. Treat yo'self!

Top tips for SELF-CARE

It's not self-indulgent; it's self-preservation

Top tips to EATING WELL
(even on a budget)

Because food is life!

Tips for EXPLORING your SEXUALITY

Just make sure you clean up afterward!

HOBBIES

The secret to living your best life!

| |
| |
| |
| |
| |
| |

TRYING NEW THINGS

After all, it's better to say, "Whoops!" than, "What if?"

Tips for FIGURING OUT WHO YOU ARE

Warning: may take a lifetime.

My best overall LIFE ADVICE

Get comfortable, cuz it's my time to shine!

www.ingramcontent.com/pod-product-compliance
Lightning Source LLC
Chambersburg PA
CBHW061146120626
46546CB00005B/1952

9 781989 884836